D1515995

MOVING AROUND THE WORLD

TRAVEL BY ROAD AND RAIL

MICHAEL POLLARD

Editorial planning
Jollands Editions

S N C F

 SCHOOLHOUSE PRESS, *Inc.*

Original copyright, © Macmillan Education Limited 1986
© BLA Publishing Limited 1986

Designed and produced by BLA Publishing Limited,
Swan Court, East Grinstead, Sussex, England.
Also in LONDON · HONG KONG · TAIPEI · SINGAPORE · NEW YORK
A Ling Kee Company

Illustrations by Chris Rothero/Linden Artists,
 Keith Duran/Linden Artists and BLA Publishing Limited
Color origination by Chris Willcock Reproductions
Printed in Italy by G. Canale & C. S.p.A. — Torino

85/86/87/88   6 5 4 3 2 1

Acknowledgements
The Publishers wish to thank the following
organizations for their invaluable assistance in the
preparation of this book.

Austin Rover
Australian Information Service, London
Canadian Pacific
General Motors (Adam Opel AG)
General Motors (Cadillac)
General Motors (Vauxhall-Opel)
Japan National Tourist Organization
Porsche cars
Renault UK
SNCF – French Railways

Photographic credits
t = top b = bottom l = left r = right

cover: ZEFA; SNCF – French Railways

4t Mansell Collection; 4b, 9b ZEFA; 11 The Bridgeman
Art Library; 14t ZEFA; 14/15, 16t The Bridgeman Art
Library; 17 Mansell Collection; 19 ZEFA; 21t 21b, 22,
23t, 23b, 24, 25 The National Motor Museum, Beaulieu;
27 Victor Hand; 29t Canadian Pacific; 29b Australian
Information Service, London; 30 ZEFA; 31t Loek
Polders; 31b ZEFA; 32t Austin Rover; 32b Loek Polders;
33t Porsche Cars; 33b General Motors (Cadillac); 34, 35t,
35b ZEFA; 36, 37t, 37b L.A.T. Photographic; 38 ZEFA;
39t SNCF – French Railways; 39b Japan National Tourist
Organization; 42 SNCF – French Railways; 43t, 43b
General Motors (Adam Opel AG); 44 Loek Polders; 45b
Japan National Tourist Organization

Note to the reader
In this book there are some words in the text which are printed in **bold** type. This shows that the
word is listed in the glossary on page 46. The glossary gives a brief explanation of words which may
be new to you.

Contents

Introduction

What would life be like if you had to walk everywhere? You can only walk about four miles per hour. It would take you two-and-one-half hours to walk ten miles, and you would be very tired by the end of your journey. However, if you traveled the same distance by road or by rail, your trip would be over soon.

Today, we travel by road and by rail for many reasons. Children frequently go to school by car or by bus. Adults sometimes **commute** to and from work by car. We go to visit friends or relatives, or we take a vacation. Some people travel away from home on **business** trips. Trucks and trains carry **freight** and mail.

▲ This old picture shows a train passing through an American city in the 1880s. As the train moved slowly through the streets, it made a lot of noise. The wheels clanged on the rails, and a bell rang all the time to tell people that the train was coming. At the crossings, a man with a flag warned people to keep out of the way.

Road and Rail

Getting from place to place was not always as easy as it is today. Until about 150 years ago, the roads were poor and there were no cars. Some people traveled on horseback or in a cart or **carriage** pulled pulled by horses. Most people walked to work. Children walked to school.

There was no rail travel before 1825. No one had ever traveled at a speed of 30 miles per hour. Many people, including doctors, thought that traveling at this speed would be bad for a person's health.

In the 1830s, the first railroads came to the towns and cities and caused a great change in people's lives. A letter could be mailed on one day and reach a distant city or town by the next day. For the first time, people who lived in cities could have fresh food brought in by train from the countryside. People could travel all over if they had money to pay the **fare**.

For many years, trains were the main means of transportation on the land. The kinds of engines used in cars and trucks were only invented about 100 years ago. At first, there were only a few cars on the roads. Then more cars and trucks were made. The roads were improved so that people could travel faster between cities.

Now we have a choice if we want to travel or send freight by land. We can use roads and railroads. We can travel part of the way by road and part of the way by rail. This book tells the story of how people travel on the land.

◀ In Tokyo, Japan, some trains run along a special kind of railroad track. The trains run on a single rail called a monorail. Electric motors turn the driving wheels. There are also monorails in France and Germany.

▶ The wheel was invented nearly 5,000 years ago. Wheels have been used for transportation ever since. Trains were invented only 150 years ago. Cars were invented after trains and have been used for only 100 years.

before 3000 BC	**The First Wheel**
	Solid wooden wheels found in Russia date from before 3000 BC
about 2000 BC	**The First Ox Cart**
	We know that the Sumerians used an ox-drawn sled about this time
about 1300 AD	**Pack Animals**
	These were used very widely in Europe in the Middle Ages and earlier in Asia
about 1500 AD	**The First Carriages**
	These were only used by nobles and rich people
1804 AD	**The First Railroad Locomotive**
	This was built by an Englishman named Richard Trevithick
1863 AD	**The First Motor Car**
	This was built by a French engineer in Paris

Wheels and Chariots

▲ Tree trunks were used as rollers to move heavy objects like this huge block of stone.

The first carts were like sleds. They did not have wheels. The carts had wooden runners, and they were pulled by oxen. When a load is pushed or pulled along the ground, a force called **friction** tries to hold it back. Friction made sleds very hard to use on uneven ground.

Long ago, people used tree trunks to help them construct buildings. When they wanted to move a heavy block of stone they used tree trunks as rollers. This idea led even further. People began to use slices of tree trunks as solid wheels.

Next, they made a simple wheelbarrow. This was a wooden box with solid wooden wheels on each side. The wheelbarrow had two handles to allow a person to wheel it along. Even now, it is far easier to wheel a load in a wheelbarrow than to drag it along the ground. Because a wheel is round, only a tiny part of it touches the ground. Therefore, there is less friction and it takes less effort to do the work.

There were no roads in early times. People used tracks that were rough and bumpy, and frequently the wheels fell off their carts. Then people found that they could join two wooden wheels with a wooden **axle**. An axle made the wheels last longer.

▶ Solid wooden wheels were used first for simple handcarts or wheelbarrows. The wheels were made by slicing tree trunks.

Animal Power

Oxen were used to pull plows and sleds. They were also used to pull carts with wheels. When the load was heavy, two or more oxen were used. Oxen and ox carts are still used today in some parts of the world. They are strong, but they are very slow. Horses are much faster. Wild horses from central Asia were used to pull light carts called **chariots**. Chariots had two wheels and were built for speed. They were first used for war. Later, they were used for hunting.

The Romans lived in a part of the world that is now called Italy. They found another use for chariots. The Romans used them for racing around a track. Thousands of Romans watched the chariot races. The winners of the races were treated as heroes.

▲ People began to use wheeled carts drawn by oxen about 4,000 years ago. The wheels of the carts were joined by an axle. The body of a cart was shaped like the letter A.

▼ The racing chariots had two wheels. The Romans stood up when they drove the chariots.

Roman Roads

The Romans ruled most of Europe and North Africa for about 400 years. They were very good builders and **engineers**. The Romans built the first real roads. They needed the roads in order to send their soldiers quickly to any part of their **empire**. They also built forts along the roads to guard the troops from attack.

There were no maps to help the Romans plan their roads. They had to mark out the **route** on the ground as they went along. First, engineers would look from the top of one hill to the next hill. Next, they lit fires and moved the fires until the fires were all in a line with one another. Finally, the engineers marked out a straight route with posts.

The Roman way of building was so good that the Roman roads ran in a straight line for a great many miles. Many of the modern roads in Europe follow the same routes used by the Romans more than 1,500 years ago. The Romans thought their empire would last forever. That is why they built their roads to last a long time.

Building a Road

The Roman roads were 24 feet wide. They were built on raised banks called **aggers**. These sloped down on each side to let water run off. Aggers were made of tightly packed chalk or clay and were covered by a layer of **flints** or stones. On top of the layer of flints or stones was another layer made up of **gravel** or large stone blocks. The Roman roads were so well made that the Roman soldiers could easily march 30 miles a day on them.

▼ The Romans built the first good roads about 2,000 years ago. First, they built up banks of earth and stone. Then, they laid the surface of the roads on top.

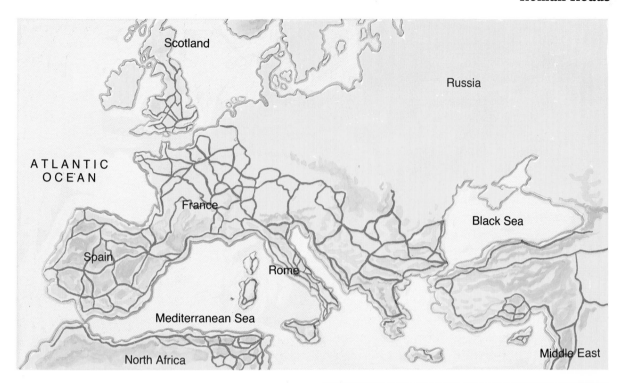

▲ The map shows some of the main roads built by the Romans. You can see that the Romans controlled most of western Europe and part of North Africa and the Middle East. The Romans went as far north as Scotland. They built good, straight roads wherever they went.

Water Supplies

The Romans also built towns, farms, and large houses called **villas**. These houses had hot and cold water. They even had a kind of central heating. It was very important for the Romans to have supplies of fresh water. They frequently brought water to their towns from a great distance.

The Romans built huge **aqueducts** to bring the water to their towns. Aqueducts were channels made of stone. If an aqueduct had to cross a valley, the Romans used curved arches set on a row of pillars. The Romans used the same method to make their road bridges as they did to make their aqueducts. Some of these Roman bridges can still be seen in parts of Europe.

▲ This Roman road looks the same today as it did 2,000 years ago. It is part of the main highway between Rome and Ostia. Ostia was the port from which Roman galleys sailed to North Africa and other parts of their empire. The road was called the Decumanus Maximus.

Carriages and Coaches

The Roman Empire did not last. By about 400 AD, the Romans had left most of the countries they had occupied. Their fine villas, forts, towns, and roads fell into ruins, and no one bothered to fix them.

The people of Europe did less traveling after the Romans had gone. If they had to travel from town to town, they went on horseback. They used old tracks and paths which were too rough and narrow for carts. Goods were carried by pack animals such as horses, donkeys, or mules. These animals carried baskets or packs slung across their backs. Up to nine animals could be roped together and led by one driver.

Wagons were used in towns. The wagons had four wheels, and they were pulled by four horses. They had canvas tops and looked very much like the wagons of the American West.

▲ The roads in Europe became too bad for carts to drive on them after the Romans left. People used pack animals instead of carts. The animals were led on old paths and tracks.

▼ The first carriages were grand vehicles. They were very heavy and had four large wheels. A carriage was drawn by four or six horses.

The most comfortable way for people to travel in towns was by **sedan chair**. This was a covered, box-like chair. Servants at the front and back lifted the chair on **shafts** and carried it along on their shoulders. Only rich people could afford to travel this way.

Carriages

About 350 years ago, horse carriages were built to carry people. The bodies of these carriages were slung on iron **springs**, which gave the passengers a smooth ride on the bumpy town streets. People who could not afford to own a carriage could hire one.

Slowly, the roads between the towns were improved. The use of carriages became more common. However, they frequently got stuck in the mud or in the snow. Sometimes their wheels were smashed by holes in the road.

▲ A stage coach carried about nine passengers. Some sat inside the coach, while others sat outside with the driver. Stage coaches stopped at stations often. Here the horses were changed, and sometimes the passengers had a meal.

The Stage Coach

The first stage coaches began to run in about 1700. These stage coaches took people across the countryside for a fare. The horses were changed every ten miles or so. A trip of 60 miles could take up to 12 hours. Bit by bit the roads were improved, and the stage coaches went faster.

Stage coaches began to run along the roads that Americans built to join their towns and cities. They carried mail as well as people. As in Europe, stage coaches were no longer used once the railroads were built.

The Great Trails

The first people who traveled by sea from Europe to America settled on the east coast. Many of those who arrived later wanted to find new land to farm. They traveled in groups, or trains, of ox-drawn wagons to the great plains of the Midwest. Dozens of wagons would set out together.

People had to take everything with them that they would need on these long journeys. They took food, clothes, bedding, and tools. For months on end, the wagons were their homes on wheels. It was a time of great adventure.

▲ A camp was made at night. The wagons were pulled up in a circle to protect the people in the wagon train. The people lighted campfires in the center of the circle and cooked their food. Then they settled down for the night.

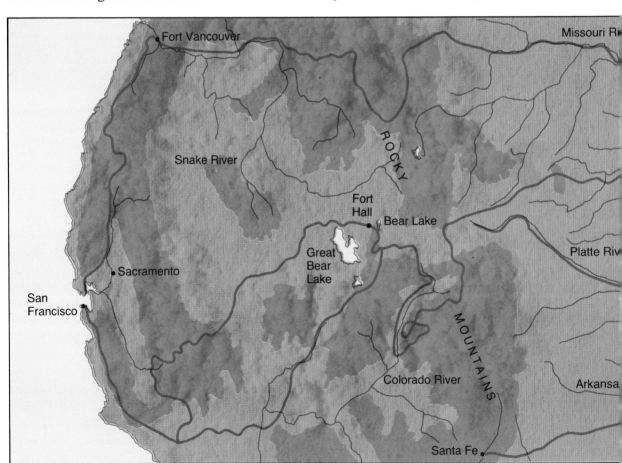

Fort Vancouver

Missouri Ri

Snake River

ROCKY

Fort Hall

Bear Lake

Great Bear Lake

Platte Riv

Sacramento

San Francisco

MOUNTAINS

Colorado River

Arkansa

Santa Fe

▲ It was always difficult taking a wagon train across a river. Sometimes, the wagons went over hidden rocks in the river and their wheels would be broken. Often, the wagons got stuck in the mud.

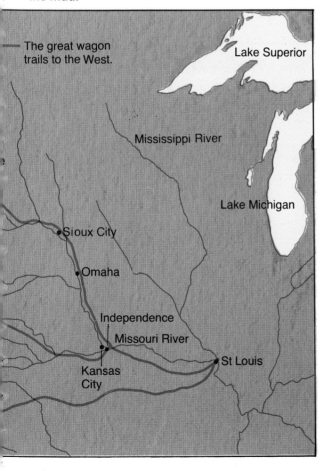

The great wagon trails to the West.

The Journey

The first great **trail** across the United States was opened in 1822. It led from Independence, Missouri, to Santa Fe, New Mexico. Twenty years later the first wagon trains crossed the Rocky Mountains to Oregon.

Each wagon train had a captain in charge and a guide to lead the way. Most days the wagon train only went about ten miles. A wagon train would sometimes take a whole day crossing a river. Wagons would sink up to their axles in mud while their drivers looked for a shallow **ford** to cross the river.

Each night the captain of the wagon train found a good place to camp. The wagons were put in a circle for safety. In the Rockies the trail was rough and full of danger. Sometimes the wagons had to go along narrow ledges. Many times there was a steep drop on one side. When a wagon wheel broke, the whole train had to stop while the wheel was repaired.

The Gold Rush

The last great trail across the United States was to California. Gold was discovered there in 1848, and the news spread fast. The next year, 1849, thousands of people set out to find gold. Most men went on their own, but some took their families with them. Most "Forty-Niners", as they were called, took the Oregon trail by wagon train as far as Fort Hall in the Rockies. From there they headed west on foot in small groups. Crossing the mountains was a difficult and dangerous journey. The "Forty-Niners" hoped to make their fortunes finding gold. Very few did, but many of the "Forty-Niners" settled in California.

Wagons continued to be used in the United States for many years. However, railroads would soon cross the **continent**. Then, the days of the great wagon trains would be over.

13

The First Railroads

Tracks made of rails were first used at coal mines. The rails were made of wood. Wagons filled with coal were pulled by horses along the tracks. The rubbing of the wagon wheels against the rails caused friction, which made it hard for the horses to pull the wagons.

Part of the solution to the problem of friction was to use iron rails instead of wooden ones. The other part of the solution was to make the wheels with a raised edge called a **flange**. The flange inside the wheels then kept the wheels on the iron track. Today, all railroad wheels have flanges.

Steam Locomotives

Steam engines had been used at mines to pump out water and prevent flooding and to lift coal or tin to the top of the mine. Richard Trevithick was the engineer at a tin mine in Cornwall, England. In 1804 he built the first steam **locomotive**. This was the first steam engine to run on an iron track.

▲ George Stephenson's Rocket was built in 1829. You can see the flange on the huge front driving wheels.

George Stephenson was also an English mine engineer. He built steam engines to use at his coal mine in northeast England.

The First Passenger Railroad

Stephenson was asked to build an engine for the first passenger railroad. He named the engine Locomotion.

In 1825 Locomotion pulled the first train that carried passengers from Darlington to Stockton in northeast England. Locomotion reached a speed of 15 miles per hour.

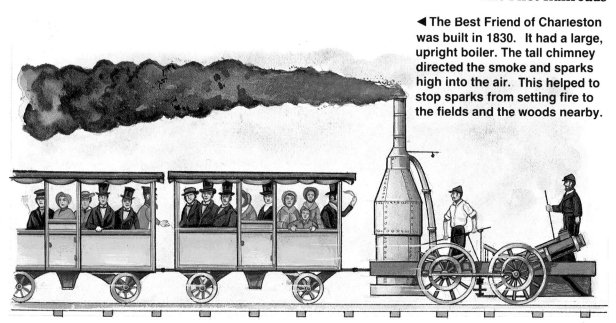

◄ The Best Friend of Charleston
was built in 1830. It had a large,
upright boiler. The tall chimney
directed the smoke and sparks
high into the air. This helped to
stop sparks from setting fire to
the fields and the woods nearby.

Stephenson was soon asked to build a new railroad to go from Liverpool to Manchester. Stephenson's locomotive was called The Rocket. It reached a speed of 29 miles per hour, and it won the prize for the best locomotive.

The South Carolina Railroad

The next year, a steam locomotive was built in New York. It was called The Best Friend of Charleston, and it used wood for **fuel**. The South Carolina Railroad opened on Christmas Day, 1830.

The Best Friend of Charleston ran a service from Charleston each day for five months. This was America's first rail service. Then, one day, the driver wanted more speed. The boiler blew up and the driver was killed. The locomotive was rebuilt. This time it was called The Phoenix. The railroad continued to run. Two years later, the South Carolina Railroad was the longest in the world.

▼ This old print shows a train on the Stockton and Darlington Railway.

Railroads Worldwide

By 1850, there were over 6,000 miles of track in Britain. The railroads spread fast. Lines ran from London to all the main cities. The Great Western Railway opened in 1841. It ran 118 miles from London to Bristol. At the time, it was the finest railroad in existence. The lines were level and straight, and the trains traveled fast. The Great Western was built so well that its bridges and tunnels are still used today.

▶ Between 1835 and 1841, Isambard Kingdom Brunel built the Great Western Railway from London to Bristol, England. This picture shows the entrance to a tunnel on this railroad. The tunnel was built so well that it is still used today.

▼ The Lafayette was one of the first American locomotives. It was built in 1837 and ran on the Baltimore and Ohio Railroad. Coal was carried in the tender behind the locomotive. The driver stood on the footplate near the huge boiler.

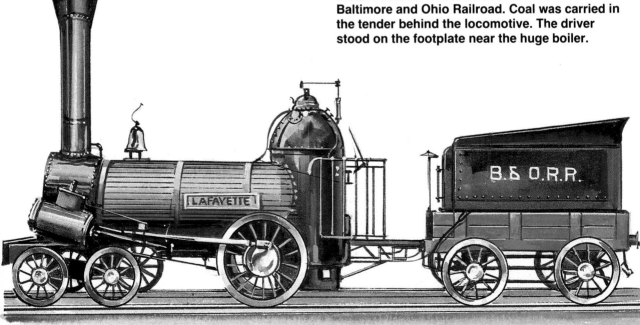

Railroads in Europe

At first, people in Europe were afraid of railroads. Then France and Germany bought engines made by Stephenson. The locomotive for the first German railroad was called Der Adler (The Eagle). It arrived from England, complete with its English driver William Wilson. He wore a top hat when he drove the train. Wilson spent the rest of his life driving trains in Germany.

The first Russian railroad also used a Stephenson locomotive. It opened in 1836 at St. Petersburg, which is now known as Leningrad.

The Golden Spike

Railroads also spread quickly in the United States. By 1850 there were nearly 3,000 miles of track. Ten years later, this number had tripled. At first, most of the lines were in the eastern states.

Then two companies set out to build a railroad across the United States from California to the plains. The Central Pacific Railroad built east from Sacramento. The Union Pacific worked west from Omaha. There were 2,000 miles of track to be laid. The route went across the **prairies** and the desert. The most difficult part of the route to build was across the Rocky Mountains.

The work began in 1864. Five years later the two tracks met at Promontory Point, Utah. It had been five years of hard work through the freezing winters and the terribly hot summers. The workmen were frequently attacked by robbers. They had to drive herds of wild buffalo off the land.

At last, it was time to drive in a spike to hold the last rail in place. A special "golden spike" was used. Everyone cheered and bells rang all over the United States.

Canada's east to west railroad opened in 1886. It was called the Canadian Pacific. Before it was built, traveling across Canada took five months. The train took only five days.

This American train of the 1880s has broken down on the line. You can see the "cowcatcher" grill on the front of the locomotive.

Building Railroads

▼ The new railroads built across the United States had to cross many rivers and valleys. The massive trestle bridges were made of timber cut in the nearby forests. These wooden bridges have now been replaced by trestle bridges made of steel.

Trains pick up speed slowly and they cannot brake sharply. They cannot climb steep slopes or turn sharp bends. For these reasons a railroad track has to be as level as possible. The curves must be gentle.

Millions of tons of earth and rock had to be moved to lay down the tracks. If there were hills in the way, **cuttings** or tunnels had to be made. **Embankments** were built up to take the lines across low-lying ground. Bridges and **viaducts** had to be built to cross rivers and valleys.

No one had ever built a railroad before.

The first railroad builders had to learn how to do it as they went along. They had no drills or trucks. They used picks, shovels, and wheelbarrows to build the first railroads.

Explosives were used to make tunnels. First, earth and rock were blasted out to make a hole. Then all the **rubble** was cleared away. At each blast, the tunnel became deeper. At the same time, however, the work became more dangerous. The blasts and rockslides caused many injuries. Some of the people working on the railroads were killed.

Bridges

Before the railroads, road bridges only had to take the weight of horses and wagons. However, trains were much heavier than horses and wagons. The bridges built to carry railroads had to be stronger and longer than any road bridge that had been built before.

Building bridges cost a lot of money. One way of cutting costs was to use materials that were close by and easy to find. For the great railroads in North America, timber was easier to find than any other material. The track was carried across rivers on **trestle** bridges made of wood.

In Europe, stone or brick was used more often than wood. Some bridges were made of stone or brick arches. Some had brick or stone supports, with frames of iron to carry the track. Other bridges were made completely out of iron.

Stations

Railroad companies spent large sums of money on the main line stations. Some of these were built like castles or **cathedrals** to look important. The smaller stations were less grand. In many parts of the world, the "station" is just a small, one-room building beside the track.

▼ One of the largest bridges in the world is the Forth rail bridge in Scotland. Built in 1890, the bridge carries a railroad track over the Firth of Forth. It has three huge spans made of steel girders.

The First Cars

For 50 years after the railroads began, horse-drawn carriages were still used on the roads. No wonder that the trains had become so popular! They were faster and more comfortable than horse-drawn carriages. There were no cars or trucks.

Road Wagons

A few people had tried building "horseless carriages" to use on the roads. The first of these carriages had steam engines. The water to make the steam was carried in tanks, and coal or wood was the fuel for the engines.

In 1769, a Frenchman named Cugnot built the first steam wagon. It was very heavy and very slow and also hard to steer. A person could walk as fast as this steam wagon.

Some of the later steam engines worked better. They were, however, still slow and hard to drive. Large numbers of steam wagons were built to carry heavy goods such as logs and coal. Some of these steam wagons were still in use 50 years ago.

Steam rollers worked very well on the roads. It did not matter that they were slow and heavy. They did their job better because of their slow speed and weight. In some parts of the world, steam rollers built 100 years ago are still in use.

A New Kind of Engine

A lighter engine was needed for cars. Engineers tried using other fuels. In 1876, a German called Nicholas Otto made a new kind of engine which used gas as a fuel. In 1885, another German, Gottlieb Daimler, made the Otto engine work better by using gasoline.

Daimler and a fellow German named Benz built cars with Otto engines. The Daimler car had four wheels and could carry four people. The Benz was lighter, had three wheels, and carried two people.

Soon many other people were making cars. Some great names are among the early car makers. Henry Ford built his first car in 1896. Three years later, Robert E. Olds made the first Oldsmobile. For many years the Oldsmobile was the best-selling car in the United States.

▼ Cugnot's steam wagon had three large cartwheels. The frame was made of great wooden beams. It had a boiler in the front which worked two cylinders. The top speed was about 2 mph.

◄ The first gasoline-driven car was built by a German named Karl Benz. It was a three-wheeler and carried two passengers. Like a bicycle, its frame was made of steel tubes, and the tires had wire spokes. The Benz could travel at 8 mph.

▼ Cars like this Fiat were seen on the roads by 1899. The Fiat could seat four people. Two of them faced backwards.

Cars for the Rich

The first cars were sold to people who were rich enough to own horses and carriages. Since many of the carriage makers began to make car bodies, many of the first cars looked like carriages. After about 1900, cars began to have a shape of their own.

In those days, you could not go to a showroom and buy one of the cars on display. You had to order your car, and then it was made for you. These early cars were made to last a long time. They had strong wooden frames. The body of the car was made of metal that was much heavier than the metal used in cars today. Seats were made of the best leather, and door handles were made of brass which shone like gold.

The Car Drivers

In most cars of that period, the drivers sat alone in front. The first cars did not have windshields. The drivers often had no roof over their heads. Only the passengers who sat in the back seat were protected from the weather.

Some rich people liked to do their own driving, but most of them had **chauffeurs**. Not only did chauffeurs have to drive the car, but they had to clean and fix the car as well. Frequently, chauffeurs were men who had worked as coachmen. Some cars had speaking tubes to allow the owners in the back seat to give orders to their chauffeurs as they drove along the road.

▼ This Mercedes was made in Germany in 1904. It could hold four people in great comfort. The passengers had some protection from the weather, but there was no windshield. The four brass headlights were run on gas. They had to be lighted one at a time. Each headlight could be twisted around in any direction. Two spare tires were carried next to the driver's seat.

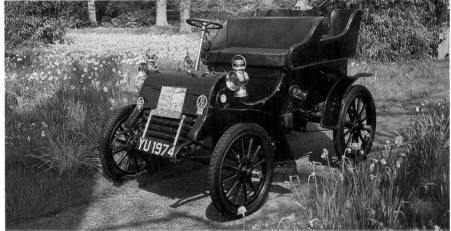

▲ This Napier was built in England in 1907. It had a huge six-cylinder engine and was very fast. The Napier was made for long trips.

▶ The Cadillac was and still is one of America's finest makes of car. This four-seater was built in 1903.

Driving Around

It was necessary to bundle up well when going for a drive in open cars. Men wore leather coats, goggles, and gloves. Women wore long linen coats. They tied their veils around their hats to keep them from blowing away. Goggles and veils were needed because the roads were so dusty.

In wet weather, it was easy to get stuck in the mud and have to push the car out. If you ran out of gasoline, you were in real trouble because there were no gasoline stations. You would have to look for a store which sold gasoline.

The speed laws were very strict in the early days of automobiles. Until 1896, the speed limit in Britain was four miles per hour. A man with a red flag had to walk in front of each car. In the United States, cities had their own speed limits which were sometimes as low as five miles per hour.

Henry Ford

One man thought that more people would buy cars if the price could be brought down to an affordable level. He was an engineer called Henry Ford. He built his first car in his spare time. The year was 1896. Six years later, Henry Ford built a factory in Detroit and started his own company to make cars.

In 1908, a new Ford car was made. It was call the Model T. The Model T was built for hard work. You could drive it almost anywhere. Spare parts were cheap and easy to replace.

Over 15 million Model T's were sold. Ford went on making them until 1927, and each year he was able to lower the price. The last Model T to be made cost only one-third of the price of the first one. This was because Henry Ford had developed a new way of making cars.

Mass Production

Before 1908, cars were built one at a time. A team of workers would finish one car and then start work on the next one. Working in this way was slow and expensive. Ford saw that the work of building a car could be split up into a number of different jobs. If each worker did a specific job on each car, the work would be done faster. This way of working is called **mass production**. The more cars that were made this way, the less each one cost the buyer, so Henry Ford was able to lower his prices.

Ford put **conveyor belts** in his factory. These slow moving belts carried the cars along. As the cars moved along each worker did one special job on every car. At the end of the production line, the cars were finished.

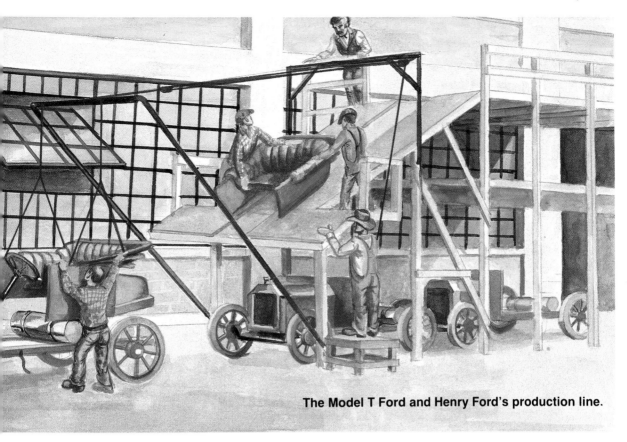

The Model T Ford and Henry Ford's production line.

Other car makers copied Ford's ideas and started mass production. Henry Ford, however, had a big headstart. The others had a long way to go to catch up. By 1926, the Ford company was the biggest producer of cars in the world, with factories in Britain and in other countries. Two million Ford cars were made each year.

No more Model T's were made after 1927, but spare parts can still be bought so that the cars can be repaired. Some people still collect Model T's. Some of these collectors are still driving their Model T cars today.

▶ After World War II, the Ford Company made a number of sports cars, as well as cars for the family. This 1955 Ford Thunderbird had a large eight-cylinder engine called a V8. In the 1960s, the Ford Mustang was the first "pony" car. The Mustang was a smaller sports car, very popular with younger people.

"The Century"

New York and Chicago are two of the largest and busiest cities in the United States. They are almost 1,000 miles apart. People who travel on business between the two cities want to travel in comfort in order to get some paperwork done on the way. They will travel regardless of what it costs them to do so. Today, business people travel by plane between New York and Chicago, but 50 years ago they traveled by train.

Back in Time

Let's go back in time. It is 2:45 in the afternoon. We are at Grand Central Station in New York. The train conductor shouts "All aboard!" At the front of the long train, the locomotive whistles in reply. All the doors are closed, and the Twentieth Century Limited begins its journey. "The Century," as the travelers call it, begins to move. We are on our way to Chicago on one of the most comfortable trains that has ever been built.

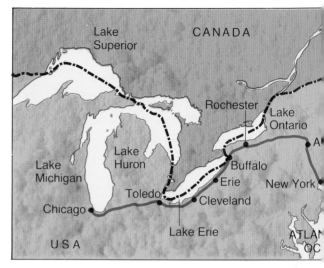

▲ The Twentieth Century Limited, or "The Century," as it was called, ran daily from New York to Chicago. In 1930, the train was made up of 13 massive cars. Together these cars weighed almost 1,000 tons.

A "Limited" train carries a fixed number of passengers. If you buy a ticket, you are certain of getting a seat. When all the seats are taken, no more tickets are sold. The Twentieth Century Limited was like a first-class hotel on wheels. It had fine dining cars and **salons**. There was plenty of room to read or work. There was even an office where people could have letters typed.

▲ After World War II, "The Century" was pulled by a diesel locomotive. Sometimes, as you can see, there were three diesel units to pull one train.

▼ This huge 4-6-4 Hudson steam locomotive was used to haul "the Century" in the 1930s. It was "streamlined" so that it could go faster.

Speeding Up

The Twentieth Century Limited first ran in 1902. In those days, the entire journey took about 20 hours. The train traveled at a speed of about 50 mph. It passed through five states and made eight stops along the way.

The New York Central and Hudson River Railroad built new and better engines for the train. By 1938, travel time between New York and Chicago had been cut to 16 hours. A morning's work could be done in New York. At noon, you could catch the train and be in Chicago in time for an early morning meeting the next day.

Now it takes less than three hours to fly from New York to Chicago. No one needs "The Century" any more, so it no longer runs. For 50 years it was one of the most famous trains in the world. Now it has become a part of railroad history.

Railroads of the World

The Twentieth Century Limited was just one of the world's great trains. It does not run any more, but many other railroads still do.

Railroads have always liked to give special names to their **luxury** trains. These trains cover long distances at top speed while the passengers ride in great comfort. **Attendants** do all they can to help the passengers.

Across the Continents

The world's great continents have famous trains running across them. The Indian Pacific runs from Perth to Sydney in Australia. The train got its name because Perth is on the Indian Ocean, and Sydney is on the Pacific. The Indian Pacific has the longest stretch of straight track in the world. It runs without a bend for 297 miles.

The Canadian runs across Canada from Montreal to Vancouver. On the way, it passes through the Rockies. Some of the coaches have domed glass roofs, which give the passengers an excellent view.

Europe's most famous train was the Orient Express. It passed through ten countries on its way from Paris, France, to Istanbul in Turkey. This train first ran in 1883. The coaches had fine furniture and thick carpets. There were also showers on board. The Orient Express has set the scene for many stories and films.

The Flying Scotsman

Each morning, a train leaves Kings Cross Station in London bound for Edinburgh in Scotland. The train is called the Flying Scotsman, and it is Britain's most famous train.

Today, the Flying Scotsman is drawn by a **diesel** locomotive, and it travels the 400 miles between London and Edinburgh in just under five hours. Until 1952, the Flying Scotsman was drawn by a steam locomotive. One day in 1938 it reached a speed of 126 miles per hour. The train still holds the world record for the fastest steam train.

Some Famous Trains				
Train	Country/Continent	Route	Distance (miles)	Average Speed (mph)
Canadian	Canada	Montreal to Vancouver	3000	43
Flying Scotsman	United Kingdom	London to Edinburgh	400	80
Indian Pacific	Australia	Perth to Sydney	2480	38
Mistral	France	Paris to Nice	676	75
Orient Express	Europe	Paris to Istanbul	1857	28
Russia	USSR	Moscow to Vladivostok	5864	30
Shinkhansen Hikari	Japan	Tokyo to Osaka	320	101
Twentieth Century Limited	USA	New York to Chicago	960	60

▲ This Canadian Pacific train is crossing a viaduct in the Rocky Mountains. In this picture, you can see three of the special domed cars. Passengers can sit in these cars to get a better view of the scenery. The silver and red cars glisten in the sun.

▶ The Indian Pacific is seen here leaving Kalgoorlie in Western Australia.

Modern Highways

The old, narrow roads were not suited for the age of the car. The cars rolling off the **assembly lines** of Detroit were bigger and faster every year. More people began to use their cars to go to work and to take vacations. The United States needed new roads that were safer, wider, and better built. The roads had to have long straight stretches with gentle slopes and curves to keep up a steady speed of traffic. They also had to be built near cities. People who wanted to drive to the center of a city left the big new road and went on into the city on a smaller, **feeder** road.

These new roads are called highways, **freeways**, **interstates**, or **expressways**.

They have at least two lanes of traffic in each direction with a dividing strip to separate the traffic going in opposite directions. Four-lane and six-lane highways are found where traffic is heavy, but most highways have two lanes. There are only a small number of entry and **exit** points to keep traffic moving. Engineers call these highways **controlled-access** roads. There are no traffic lights or crossroads on highways, and slow vehicles such as farm tractors are not allowed to use them.

Other countries also built new highways. In the 1930s, the Germans opened their first fast highway. They called it an **autobahn**. These highways were **banked** and designed for speed. They were also built to take the German army quickly from one place to another. In France, the new high speed roads are called **autoroutes**. The Italians call their highways **autostrada**.

◀ The junction between two roads or highways is sometimes called an interchange. It is designed so drivers can change from one highway to another at a steady speed without any danger. This interchange is in San Diego, California.

▶ There are tollgates on many of the French turnpikes. A green light above the gate tells drivers that they can pay and drive through the gate. Gates with a red cross above them are closed.

Construction

The best highways have a cement-concrete base strengthened with steel. The road surface on the top is a mixture of fine sand, filler, and **asphalt**. In some places, part of the cost of building the roads is paid by the drivers who pay a **toll** to travel on them. The roads are called **toll roads** or **turnpikes**.

▼ Many of the German turnpikes have "cloverleaf" junctions. You can see from this photo why they are called cloverleaf junctions.

Changing Direction

Fast-moving traffic must be able to enter or exit a highway safely. Each **junction** is built in such a way that traffic can exit or enter without crossing in front of oncoming traffic. Exit or entry lanes may go over the highway on **overpasses**. The lanes may go underneath a highway on **underpasses**. The pattern of some junctions looks like the outline of a giant four-leaf clover and is called a "cloverleaf."

Cars Today

Today, there are over 200 million cars on the world's roads. Some people choose cars which are economical to run, while others want speed and comfort. People's needs change from time to time, and they change their cars for new **models**. Most people feel that they want to have a car that is different from the one next door.

Every year the automobile industry brings out new models. They change the **design** to make the cars look better. Extras are added to keep the new models up-to-date. By providing more comfort, luxury, and safety they hope they will sell more cars.

Economy Cars

Some small cars can go more than 42 miles on one gallon of gasoline. These are known as **economy** cars. British Leyland's Mini Metro and the Renault 4 are two such models. Economy cars are especially popular in Europe. People take shorter trips than in the United States. Economy cars are inexpensive to run and easy to park because they are small. They may not not be as comfortable to drive on longer journeys as larger cars are.

Family Cars

There are more family cars on the road than any other type. They can seat four or five people in comfort. Plenty of baggage can be carried in family cars.

Large companies like Ford and Nissan keep their **production lines** running by making cars to suit the family's needs. In Europe, these cars are mostly smaller than those used in the United States. In the United States the distances are longer and the fuel is cheaper than in Europe.

▲ The Mini Metro is a small British car. It is very inexpensive to operate and easy to park.

▶ The Citroen BX is a medium-sized family car made in France. Some of the body panels are made of plastic. This makes the Citroen lighter and easier to repair.

▶ The Porsche 911 is made at Stuttgart in West Germany. The Porsche Company only builds and sells sports cars. They have small engines but they go very fast. They hold the road well on corners. These cars got their name from Dr. Ferdinand Porsche, who was a race car designer.

Luxury Cars

Luxury cars are often owned by people with a lot of money or by companies. The engines are larger and they use much more gasoline. Luxury cars like the Rolls-Royce, Lincoln, and Cadillac are often used by important people. They are sometimes driven around by chauffeurs.

Sports Cars

Many people dream of owning a sports car. Sports cars like the Ferrari, the Alfa Romeo and the Corvette are exciting to drive. They are sleek, low, and very fast, and they also use a lot of gasoline. Even so, most of us would still like to own a sports car at some time in our lives.

◀ This photograph shows a 1985 Cadillac, a Fleetwood Brougham. It is a very large luxury car and uses a lot of gasoline. Cars that use a lot of gasoline are sometimes known as "gas guzzlers."

Giants of the Road

▼ American truck drivers like to keep their trucks clean and shiny. This large Peterbilt truck has a sleeping area at the back of the cab. The two exhaust pipes make the exhaust fumes go high up in the air. This keeps the exhaust fumes away from people on the ground.

As the new highways were built, trucks became larger and larger. Now the trucks have taken much of the freight trade away from the railroads. Giant trucks carry goods throughout the United States. Long-distance trucks cross Europe from Britain to the Middle East.

Most of these huge trucks are **articulated**, which means that they are made up of two parts. In front is the **tractor unit**. In the tractor is the large engine and the driver's cab. The tractor is attached to the back part called the trailer. In some countries a second trailer can be added on to make a train of trailers.

Articulated trucks are easier to drive and park than trucks made in one piece. They

can be unhitched to start the next job before the trailer is unloaded. In the United States, some drivers own the tractor unit, but not the trailer. A driver can keep busy and earn a good living with just one tractor.

Behind the driver in a tractor are the sleeping quarters. These have bunk beds. Some even have a stove, refrigerator and a TV set.

Juggernauts

Juggernaut is an Indian word which means a huge cart. The word is used in Europe for giant trucks. Like American truckers, British drivers can sleep in their cabs when they have to.

If drivers start out from Britain, they have to cross the English Channel. They go by sea ferry. Large ferries can carry up to 60 juggernauts. Then, a long trip to the Middle East may take the drivers through ten countries. The rules of the road for each country must be learned. The British drive on the left side of the road, so they must remember to drive on the right once they cross the English Channel.

The Outback

In the middle of Australia is desert land called the **outback**, or back country. The largest trucks in the world are used there. One truck may have three or more trailers. The distances between the few towns are so great that the drivers may take days to get from one town to the next.

▲ Containers are brought by sea to Tilbury Docks in London. The elevated platform on the right of the picture is used to lift the containers off the ships and onto the trucks.

▼ This picture shows a line of heavy trucks, or "road trains," moving across the Australian outback. Trucks often travel in groups or convoys in case one truck breaks down in the desert.

Grand Prix

The first auto races were held on public roads. The races were noisy and dangerous. There were many accidents. It was decided shortly afterwards that auto races must take place on special tracks.

"Grand Prix" is French for "big prize." The first Grand Prix was held at Le Mans, France in 1906. The roads were closed to the public for two days during the race. The cars had to complete 780 miles in just two days. It was more than just a sporting event. Automakers entered their cars in the race to advertise their products. They used the race to test and improve their cars.

In 1907, the first auto racing track was built at Brooklands near London. At that time, people thought that nothing on earth could go faster than 130 mph. The curves on the track were banked so that as the cars went around the track they went up the banking. Later, when cars went faster 130 mph, some went over the top of the bank, and the drivers were killed. Now racing tracks are designed for higher speeds.

Indianapolis

The most famous race in the world was the Indianapolis 500. It was first run in 1911. Ray Harroun won it in a Marmon Wasp. His speed was 75 mph. In 1925, Peter de Paulo was the first to win the race at a speed of over 100 mph. The Indianapolis 500 now counts as a Grand Prix event in the United States.

▼ A pit-stop at the Indianapolis 500. Here every second counts. The tires can be changed and the car can be back in the race in under 10 seconds.

Formula 1

Early racing cars were very heavy. They had huge engines. Usually the car with the largest engine won the race. Racing officials decided to group racing cars in classes to prevent the cars with big engines from having an unfair advantage. Each class is called a **formula**. The Formula rules limit the size of the engine and the width and weight of the car. Formula 1 cars are the fastest racing cars. Only Formula 1 cars can take part in Grand Prix races.

Ten countries throughout the world have Grand Prix races which count in the world championship. The top Formula 1 drivers take part in all the races. They earn points for their finishing places in each race. The driver with the most points is named world champion for the year. The first American winner was Phil Hill, in 1961.

▲ This photo shows car racing in the 1930s at Brooklands in England. The cars in this picture are, from left to right, Austin, Riley, Bentley, and MG. They are traveling at about 100 mph.

▼ The start of the Portugal Grand Prix, 1985.

High Speed Trains

High **S**peed **T**rains are called HSTs. They should really run on special tracks. HST's need long, straight stretches with very gentle curves. In most countries of the world, HST's use the old track **smoothed out**.

In Britain, the HSTs are called "125s." They can reach a speed of 125 mph. The first HST service started running from London to Bristol in 1976. An even faster British train is called the **A**dvanced **P**assenger **T**rain, or APT. It can reach a speed of 155 mph. The engineers have had trouble getting the APT ready for use.

America's first HST is called the Metroliner. It goes from New York to Washington in three hours, at a speed of 75 mph. Once the track is smoothed out, it will be able to reach 160 mph. Canada's HST is called the Turbo Train. The coaches **tilt** to help the train go around the curves. The Turbo runs from Montreal to Toronto. It takes just over four hours to do the 335-mile journey.

▼ **The Canadian HST runs between Montreal and Toronto. It is called the Turbo, or LRC. The letters stand for Light, Rapid, and Comfortable. The LRC has a top speed of about 125 mph.**

French HSTs

The French State Railways built a special track for their HST. The train goes 265 miles from Paris to Lyons in just two hours. Their train is called the TGV. The letters TGV stand for **T**rain **G**rand **V**itesse, French for high speed train. The top speed of the TGV is 188 mph.

The Tokaido Express

Japan's HST also runs on a special track. Most people call the Tokaido Express the "Bullet Train" because of its shape and speed. The Bullet Train takes about three hours to cover the 320 miles from Tokyo to Osaka. Its top speed is 156 mph.

The Japanese are now building a Bullet Train network all over their country. There are even plans to build a line linking the mainland to Japan's northern-most island of Hokkaido.

▲ This picture shows the French TGV at top speed. The TGV travels on the fast stretches of track at a speed of 168 mph.

▼ Japanese Bullet trains have a total weight of 850 tons. There are 16 cars on each train.

The record breakers

1825 The Rocket United Kingdom	
1848 The Great Britain United Kingdom	
1893 Empire State Express No 999 USA	
1938 Mallard United Kingdom	
1981 TGV France	
1979 Maglev test train Japan	

| kph | 100 | 200 | 300 | 400 |
| mph | | 100 | 200 | |

1885 Benz Tricycle Germany	Karl Benz
1899 Jamais Contente France	Jenatzy
1904 Gobron-Brillie France	Louis Rigolly
1927 Sunbeam United Kingdom	Henry Segrave
1947 Napier-Railton United Kingdom	
1964 Spirit of America USA	
1970 The Blue Flame USA	
1983 Thrust 2 United Kingdom	

40

Who is the fastest on road and rail? Makers of cars and locomotives have always wanted to see their names at the top of the list. For many years trains were the fastest vehicles on earth. By the time the first car was built, trains had reached a speed of 70 mph. The first cars had a top speed of 10 mph. Even at that speed, people thought they were dangerous. Cars, however, soon became faster than trains and have stayed ahead ever since.

Railroad Records

The passengers who have traveled fastest by rail are the Japanese. In 1979, a train on a test track in Japan went over 321 mph.

The fastest regular train service is also in Japan; it is the Bullet Train. France holds the record for the fastest train on an ordinary track.

Land Speed Records

All the holders of land speed records drove cars which had to be specially built. They are only able to carry a driver. The cars had different types of engines. In 1970, an American, Gary Gabelich, drove at 631 mph. His car, Blue Flame, had a rocket engine. Then in 1983, Richard Noble, a British driver, broke Gabelich's record in his Thrust 2. Thrust 2 was powered by a jet engine.

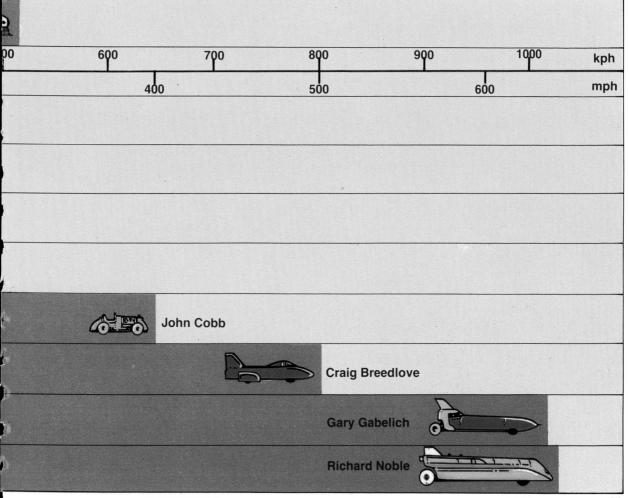

Safety on Road and Rail

A train weighs several hundred tons and travels at very high speeds. It cannot stop suddenly or swerve. Yet travel by rail is safer then travel by road.

Railroad Signals

The speed of the first railroad trains frightened people, causing the need for safety signals. At first it was decided that trains should be kept apart from each other by a time interval. A second train would not start out until a fixed time after the first had left. If the first train broke down, however, the plan did not work.

The "block" system was better. Each line is divided into sections. Only one train is allowed in one section at one time. A signal warns the driver if there is a train in the section ahead. Then, the driver must stop until the signal shows "all clear." The "block" system is still used on most railroads.

Many trains are also fitted with **automatic** warning systems. If a train passes a signal set at "danger," the train brakes automatically. The same sort of system can be used to slow a train down if it is going too fast.

Many modern trains are equipped with "the dead man's handle," which the driver holds down to keep the train moving. If the driver lets go of the handle, the train stops. Therefore, if the driver collapses or dies, the train is unable to move.

▼ The French rail system is up-to-date. Information about the trains is fed into computers at the traffic control centers. There are many of these centers throughout France. A large screen shows the railroad track. This lights up to show where each train is and where it is going.

Safety on the Road

It is not easy to make travel by road safe. There is little that can be done to stop every driver from breaking road laws. There are not enough police on the roads and highways to watch every driver.

Cars, however, can be made to run more safely even if the drivers can't. When automakers build a new model, they test the car by crashing it. They set the car to run into a wall at different speeds. There are dummies to simulate people inside. The automakers can see what happens to the dummies when the crash takes place.

Most new cars are now built with "safety shells" around the passengers. The shell will absorb the first shock of a crash. In most countries, people in the front seat have to wear seat belts. In some countries, people in the back must also wear seat belts.

▲ New car models are tested with dummies inside them. The car is made to crash head-on into a wall. In this picture, the front of the car has crumpled, but the "passengers" are safe.

▼ The steel frame at the front and at the back of the car is designed to crumple and absorb the shock from a crash. The passengers are protected by a strong, rigid steel frame around them.

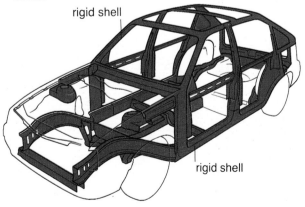

rigid shell

rigid shell

Looking Ahead

As we look back through the history of travel by road and rail, we come across "milestones." Each milestone marks an event where the human race has made a big stride forward. The invention of the wheel, the steam locomotive, and Otto's new engine were all great events in transportation.

Some people think that the year 2000 may bring another great event. By that year the world's oil supplies may soon run out, and the shortage of oil will force us to find a new way of making cars run. Cars are a part of our lives. We would not want to do without them.

New Cars for Cities

Some people think that the electric car is the car of the future. For many years, people have been trying to build a car that would run a long way on electric **batteries**. Up to now, electric cars cannot go very fast or very far. These electric batteries are too heavy and need to be recharged every 20 miles or so. What is needed is a small, long-lasting battery.

It may be that one day you can go to work by electric car. The batteries will be charged at home while you sleep. There will be a place for you to recharge your battery where you work in order to get you home again.

It may be that someone in the future will invent a new kind of battery, or even a new kind of engine. Then there will be no noise and no exhaust fumes to spoil our towns and cities.

◄ The electric car is still a vehicle of the future in most parts of the world. The Dutch people, however, are already driving these cars. Small two-seaters can be rented for use in Amsterdam. They run on batteries and are kept in special parking areas.

Trains of the Future

The trains of the future may be here already. We may see many more trains such as the Japanese Bullet train and the French TGV. One new idea for faster and more efficient trains is the **levitation** train. Most people call it the **maglev** train. This word stands for **mag**netic **lev**itation, which means raised by **magnets**. This train has no wheels. It uses a special track which is equipped with magnets. There are also magnets on the train. When the magnets are switched on, the train is pulled along. Some maglev test lines have been built. There is one short line used in Britain. It links Birmingham Airport with the nearby National Exhibition Center.

The maglev idea works well on lines with no junctions. It has not yet been worked out how maglev could switch from one line to another.

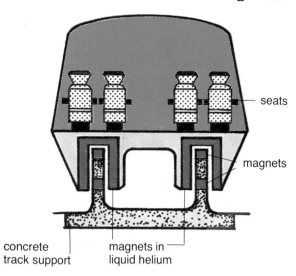

seats

magnets

concrete track support

magnets in liquid helium

▲ Maglev trains can travel very fast. However, they have to have a special track which is expensive to build.

▼ By the year 2000, we may see maglev trains like this one in many of the world's cities. They will cause no pollution and make little noise.

Glossary

agger: a chalk or clay bank on which the Romans built their roads.

aqueduct: a channel built to carry water. The first aqueducts were built by the Romans and were made of stones or bricks.

articulated: describes a large truck with a trailer which is jointed between the tractor and the trailer.

asphalt: a thick, black liquid made from oil. Roads are covered with asphalt.

assembly line: a row of machines or workers, working one after the other to make something.

attendant: a person who looks after the needs of passengers on trains.

autobahn: the German name for a road specially built to carry fast traffic.

automatic: describes a machine or process that works on its own. Does not need human help.

autoroute: the French name for a road specially built to carry fast traffic.

autostrada: the Italian name for a road specially built to carry fast traffic.

axle: a wooden or metal rod which joins two wheels.

banked: a bend on a road or car racing track which has been built so that the surface slopes upwards and outwards.

battery: a device for making electricity, consisting of two or more cells.

business: any job or activity done to make a living, such as making things, providing services, or buying and selling goods.

carriage: a wheeled vehicle for carrying people, usually drawn by horses.

cathedral: a large and important church.

chariot: a light, two-wheeled cart drawn by one or more horses. Chariots were used by the Romans for war and for racing.

chauffeur: a person whose job is to drive someone in a car.

commute: to travel daily to and from work by car or public transportation.

continent: one of the large land masses on earth. There are seven continents.

controlled-access: describes a road which has only a few points where traffic can join or leave the road.

conveyor belt: a moving belt which carries cars or other things from one part of a factory to another.

cutting: a wide channel cut through a hill for a road or railroad.

design: the way something is made or built and how it looks.

diesel: a type of engine that burns heavy oil. The diesel engine was invented by Rudolf Diesel.

economy: the careful use of something, such as fuel, to avoid wasting it and to save money.

embankment: a bank of earth on which railroads and roads are built.

empire: a number of countries under one ruler.

engineer: a person who builds large works such as roads. Also a person who works or takes care of machines.

exit: the way out from a road or building.

explosive: gunpowder or other material used to blow up something.

expressway: the name for a road specially built to carry fast traffic.

fare: the price of a ticket for a journey.

feeder: a road or railroad which takes traffic on to larger or more important roads or railroads.

flange: the raised edge on the inside of a train wheel.

flint: a kind of stone which is hard but splits easily.

ford: a shallow place in a river where people, animals, and vehicles can cross.

formula: a class of racing car.

freeway: the name for a road specially built to carry fast traffic. An expressway.

freight: the goods carried by any form of transport.

friction: the rubbing of one surface against another surface. Friction slows things down.

fuel: a material burned in engines to provide power for movement.

gravel: small stones.

interstate: a highway running between two or more states.

juggernaut: the name given to a large truck.

junction: the place where roads or railroads join.

levitation: lifting above the ground.

locomotive: an engine which pulls a train.

luxury: very great comfort.

maglev: a new kind of train which does not have wheels. Maglev is short for **mag**netic **lev**itation, which means lifted above the ground by magnets.

magnet: a piece of iron or steel made to attract or repel another piece of iron or steel.

mass production: a way of making things in a factory where each worker does the same job on a part of each thing being made.

model: a product with a particular design. New models of cars are made each year.

outback: an isolated part of the country, especially in Australia, which has few people or towns.

overpass: a bridge which carries a road or railroad over a large road.

prairie: a large area of grassland without trees.

production line: a way of arranging people or machines in a factory one after another so that they can efficiently do their part in making something.

route: the way from one place to another. Routes are shown on maps.

rubble: broken bricks and stone.

salon: a room on a train or a ship where any passenger can sit in comfort.

sedan chair: a covered, box-like chair for one person which is carried on two poles by other people.

shaft: a long handle or pole which is used to carry or pull something along.

smoothed out: the words used to describe railroad track that has been made straighter and smoother so that trains can travel at a high speed.

spring: a metal strip or coil. As it bends gently up and down, the spring reduces the amount of shock passengers feel when a vehicle changes direction or hits bumps in a road or track.

tilt: to slope or lean.

toll: the amount of money charged to use a road or a bridge.

toll road: a road which drivers of vehicles must pay to use. A turnpike.

tractor unit: the front part of an articulated truck. It contains the engine and the driver's cab.

trail: a path through a forest or mountain region. Also a route used by people or cattle passing through a wilderness.

trestle: a wooden or metal criss-cross framework that supports a road or railroad bridge.

turnpike: a road which drivers of vehicles must pay to use. A toll road.

underpass: a tunnel which carries a road or railroad under another road.

viaduct: a long, high bridge on a row of arches which carries a road, railroad, or aqueduct.

villa: a large house built by the Romans with outbuildings and farmland nearby.

Index